William Bolcom

The Garden of Eden
Four Rags for Two Pianos

ISBN 978-0-634-07304-5

EDWARD B. MARKS MUSIC COMPANY / Exclusively Distributed By HAL•LEONARD® CORPORATION

7777 W. BLUEMOUND RD. P.O. BOX 13819 MILWAUKEE, WI 53213

The Garden of Eden was originally published in its solo piano version in 1974. The four rags that make up the suite tell the story of the Fall in ragtime. **Old Adam**, a "Chicken Scratch" recalling the animal dances of the 1900s, contains a reminiscence of Chris Smith's 'teens hit "Ballin' the Jack." **The Eternal Feminine** has a harmonically devious third strain that calls up the Mystery of Woman. **The Serpent's Kiss** notably recalls the ragtime tradition of heel-stomping and knocking on the wood of the piano, and adds to this the clicking of tongues! **Through Eden's Gates** conjures the image of Adam and Eve calmly cakewalking their way out of Paradise. The latter two rags were arranged by the composer for Richard and John Contiguglia's 1994 Helicon recording, *Grainger and Bolcom*. The first two rags were arranged by the composer expressly for this publication.

"The Serpent's Kiss" and "Through Eden's Gates" for Two Pianos are currently available on CD recorded by Elizabeth and Marcel Bergmann

William Bolcom
Music for Two Pianos
Naxos American Classics 8.559244

Bolcom's Complete Rags for Solo Piano available on CD recorded by John Murphy

William Bolcom
The Complete Rags for Piano
Albany Records
Troy 325/26

THE GARDEN OF EDEN
Four Rags for Two Pianos
I. OLD ADAM
Two Step

WILLIAM BOLCOM (1969)
Arranged for two pianos
by the composer

TRIO

Swing out!

II. THE ETERNAL FEMININE
Slow Drag

WILLIAM BOLCOM (1969)
Arranged for two pianos
by the composer

Slow march tempo (♪ = 100), *slightly swung*

light Ped.

III. THE SERPENT'S KISS
Rag Fantasy

WILLIAM BOLCOM (1969)
Arranged for two pianos
by the composer

Fast, diabolical (♩ = 96, or faster)

optional heel stomps

N.B. This repeat (mm. 9-24) optional

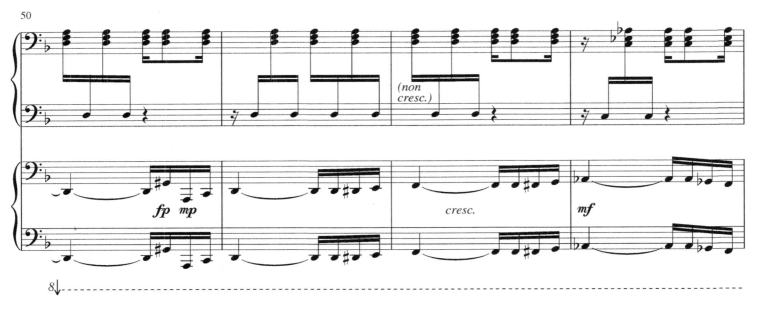

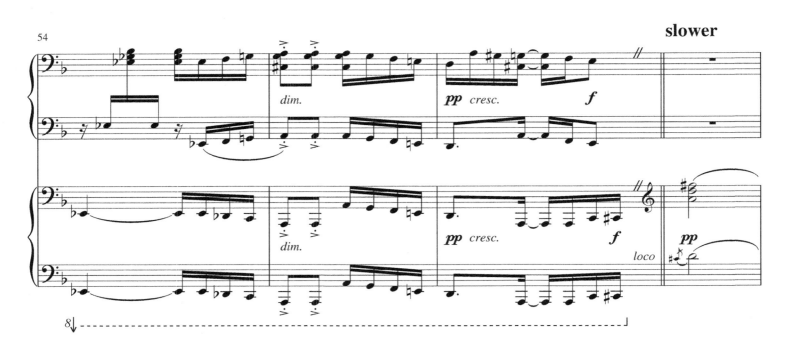

Stoptime (♩ = 104)

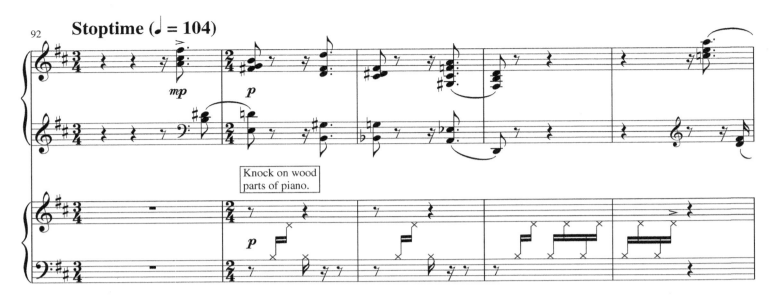

Knock on wood
parts of piano.

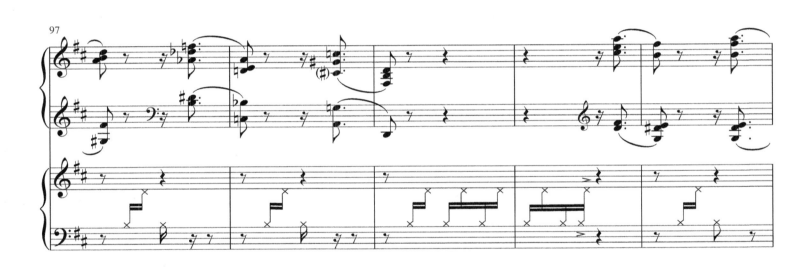

Tempo I

Now! Let go!

Slow March tempo

flat of
hand on
low keys

take silently

A tempo

IV. THROUGH EDEN'S GATES
Cakewalk

WILLIAM BOLCOM (1969)
Arranged for two pianos
by the composer

Leisurely, simply (♪ = 90)

* add "G" on D.S. 𝄉

poco allarg.

A shade slower